£6.95

Hoffnung's
ACOUSTICS

Books by
GERARD HOFFNUNG

Hoffnung's
Acoustics

GERARD HOFFNUNG

LONDON 2000

First published 1959
jointly by Dennis Dobson Ltd
and Putnam & Co Ltd

2nd impression September 1960
3rd impression October 1962
4th impression September 1965
5th impression December1968
6th impression December 1972
7th impression May 1978
8th impression May 1978 (Paperback)
and subsequently re-published by
Souvenir Press from 1983

This edition published by
The Hoffnung Partnership
44 Pilgrims Lane
London NW3 1SN

Copyright © The Hoffnung Partnership 2000

ISBN 1 903643 05 8

Cover and book design
Vera Brice and Leslie Robinson

Printed and bound in Great Britain
by St Edmundsbury Press
Blenheim Industrial Park, Newmarket Road
Bury St Edmunds, Suffolk, IP33 3TU

For
DR HOWARD FERGUSON

---■ ● ■---

Acknowledgements

Grateful thanks are due to Emily Hoffnung for her contribution
to this book, and also to its designers and printers for the
infinite care and consideration they have taken in its production.

Foreword

The spelling of the surname Hoffnung often, understandably, leaves people quite baffled. Even after my failed, lengthy attempts to go through the name letter by letter, 'Hoffnug' or 'Hoffmung' still regularly appear on some correspondence while 'Hossdung' and 'Halflung' are more imaginative variations.

However, occasionally when the spelling is spot on, or the name crops up in conversation, the next question will more likely be, 'Any relation to Gerard?' What is so inspiring is not only the sheer delight expressed by the inquirer when I admit that Gerard was my father, but also the fact that he was loved by people in so many walks of life other than in the worlds of music and art. As a sculptor, I used to go to a builders' merchants in the east end of London whose owner was a true Hoffnung fan, as was the chap in the second-hand furniture shop on the Old Kent Road who, on selling me a plans chest, informed me that he had all the Hoffnung records and books. Once, when the car broke down, the AA switchboard operator recounted his fond memories of having attended the same Quaker Meeting as my father in the early nineteen fifties.

I never knew my father so these little anecdotes which appear out of the blue are especially magical to me and emphasize what an extraordinary character he must have been.

Emily Hoffnung

The Keyboard

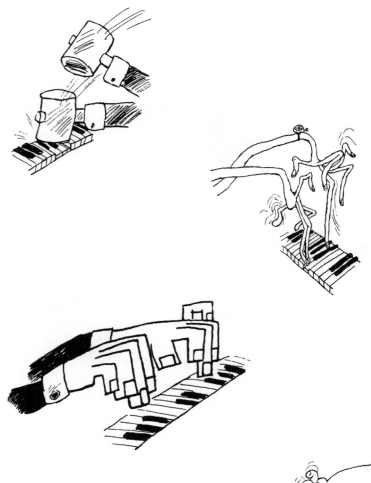

Liszt

Schönberg

A Fugue

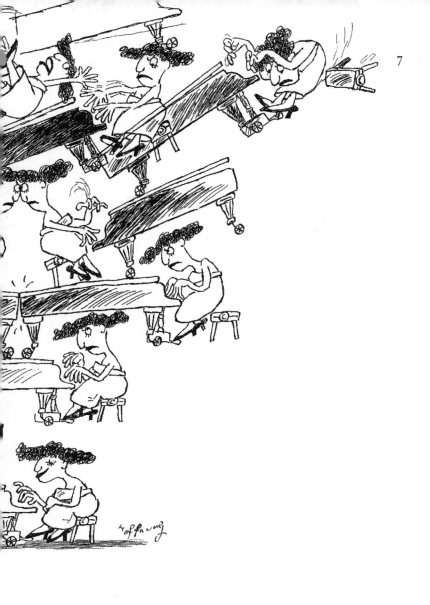

8

de Falla

Boulez

Webern

The Art of Listening

Piano

PP *con sordina*

Musique Concrète

G.H.

Noises

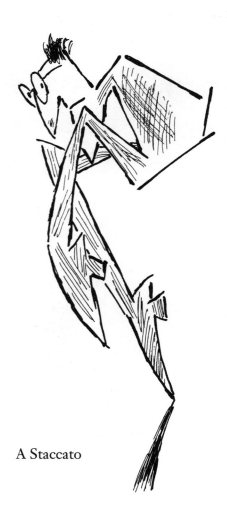

A Staccato

A Legato

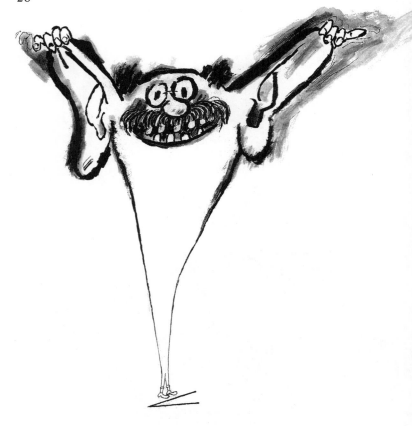

A Crescendo

A Diminuendo

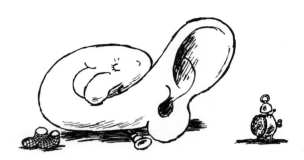

A Rest

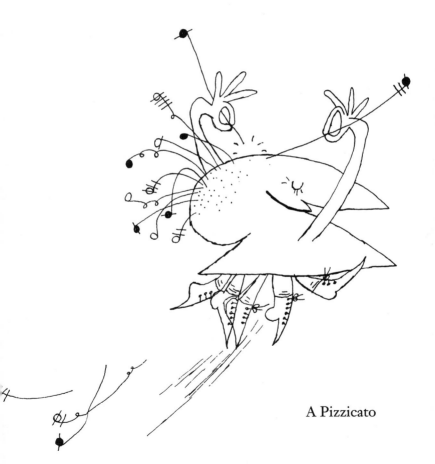

A Pizzicato

A Cadenza

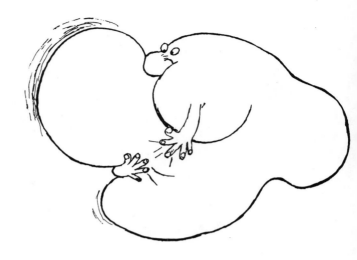

A Muted Blow

An Oompah

An Arpeggio

A Drum-roll

A Ping

A Thud

A Chord

A Discord

A Hum

A Glissando

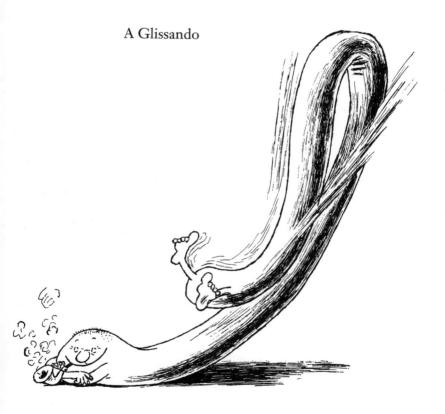

A Tutti

Union Members

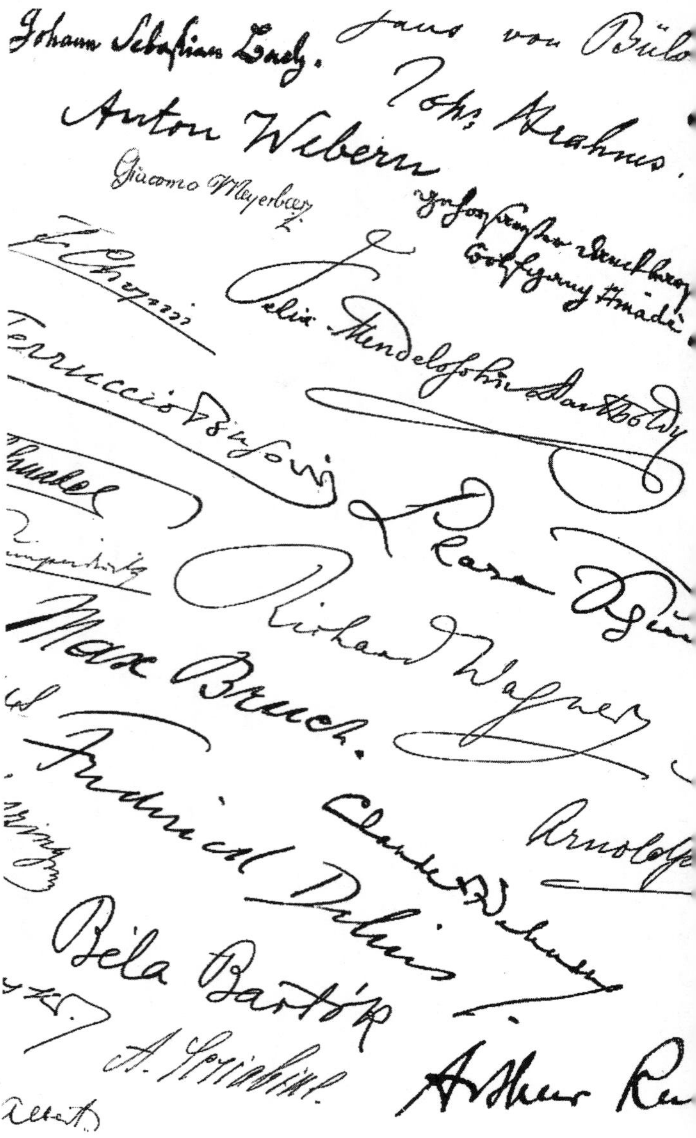

Johann Sebastian Bach. Hans von Bülo

Anton Webern

Joh. Brahms.

Giacomo Meyerbeer

Wolfgang Amadé

F. Chopin

Felix Mendelssohn Bartholdy

Ferruccio Busoni

Clara

Max Bruch.

Richard Wagner

Frederick Delius

Claude Debussy

Arnold

Béla Bartók

A. Scriabine

Arthur Ru

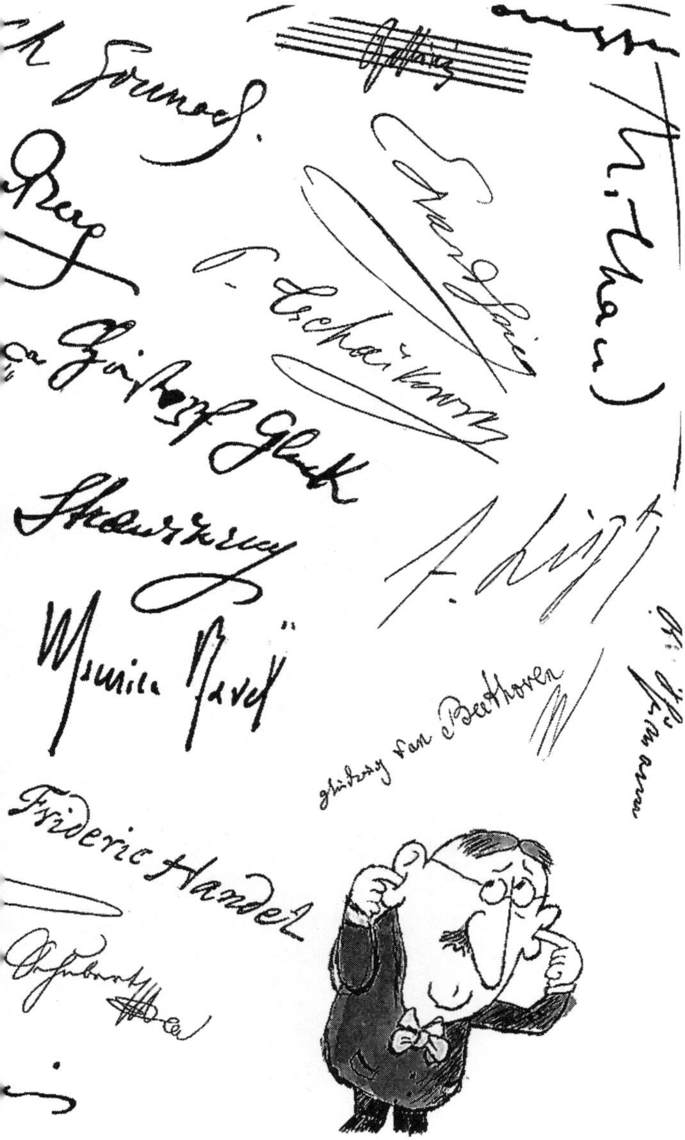
Frideric Handel
van Beethoven
Gluck